Follow–Haswed

—

Laura Walker

Apogee Press
Berkeley · California
2012

Many thanks to the editors of *Fact-Simile* and *Ambush*, where some of these poems first appeared.

Many thanks also to the amazing students I've been lucky to work with over the years—getting to know you and your writing has been a privilege. Thanks also to Megan Pruiett, Todd Melicker, Susanne Dyckman, Steve Hemenway, and Sharon Osmond, for all the kitchen-table conversations.

And heartfelt gratitude to Ed Smallfield and Valerie Coulton, for the many years of support and inspiration. Thank you.

Cover Art: "Wetlands," by Alexander Korzer-Robinson, used with the artist's permission.

Book cover and interior design by Philip Krayna at NKD
www.nkdesigngroup.com

ISBN 978-0-9851007-2-8. Library of Congress Catalog Card Number 2012905974.

Published by Apogee Press, 2308 Sixth Street, Berkeley CA, 94710.
www.apogeepress.com

Table of Contents

fraught : 7

gale : 8

furlough : 9

fraying : 10

fugue : 11

follow : 12

gallop : 13

give : 14

green : 15

gratitude : 17

give : 18

fraught : 19

gibber : 20

goblin : 21

gap : 22

goblin : 23

gorge : 24

fraternal : 25

gentle : 26

go : 27

fraught : 32

gentle : 33

haswed : 34

free : 35

go : 36

godwit : 37

go : 38

girl : 39

go : 40

give : 42

freckle : 43

girth : 44

go : 45

gain : 46

gap : 48

glide : 49

give : 50

furlong : 51

friend : 53

follow : 55

gibbous : 57

girl : 58

go : 59

God : 68

girl : 69

generate : 71

furlough : 73

go : 74

force : 75

halve : 77

gentle : 78

gibbous : 79

goose : 80

gradation : 81

gentleness : 82

gorge : 83

gap : 84

free : 85

girl : 86

fraught : 87

forget : 88

gorge : 89

for Mark

Note on the text:

These are collaged poems: each poem is composed
of fragments of a single entry from Volume VI of the
Oxford English Dictionary, "Follow–Haswed." The text
includes etymologies, usage notes, definitions, and
quotations.

Titles are the entry words. Line breaks indicate a jump
within the *OED* text.

fraught

Christ

to be cedar she was
in any storm or weather
any Strangers Ship

weary

she long'd to see
in any storm or weather
sleep

any Strangers Ship
Utensils of War
intricate

tossed bark over the water

gale

not to have survived

to sing;

furlough

believe
leave
give leave
and leave

leave
absence

to be borne about in a black box

three months
in their pockets

a soldier

fraying

of a deer
mischief from light words
tree or

ravellings

fugue

being lost by not being heard

the two start together

elderly market women
in a compass

a flight from one's own

all proportions
travel
one after another

none perhaps is so important
seizure
those strange excursions

twenty years earlier
he was in danger

follow

for more than forty years
I used to come to him in the field

into the path
to follow him

he was young

heavy

come
if you can

despair
has flown

against which
a soldier

gallop

these letters
a more open part of the forest

as necessary as
broad salt water

he was hurrying

at this pace

superseded
shoulder

a fast powerful boat

this is called
origin

to mingle with the broad
cursorily

your spleen and your rage
simple boiling

gentler and more promising
(a space)

the end
again
(a space)

give

the dead pull (so different to the spring

green

between blue and
nature, permission
to proceed.

questioning of passengers
it now seems sadly obvious

of the sea
the gifted

a beautiful dress
gold as the stone
a permanent farm road

the spirit
resembling a meadow

some green Christmas
halted and consulted

natural moisture, the children, full of
many a long year
one is cabbage-looking

-shaded, -shadowed
of milk

-throated
of a mother

whilst one side of the bone is broken the other is only bent

-curtained, -leaved

merely salted
diseased

-twined
-veined

who went on, still looking

-bodied, -bordered, -breasted

to be clothed
baffled

so carelessly greened

gratitude

birds of diverse kind
done to me

moveables restored
done to me

grace
done to me
hands

adhered

do something

an instance

give

of water in a river when you look across it

fraught

of a boat

Christ

gibber

at the strange sight of a boat
the blank space

himself by the fire-side

the river
but rougher
he might be near
led across
for the night

these are the hollows

wilderness

speak rapidly
the written form
the Roman streets

ghosts
overhead
demons, filthy and foul
can rise

a hunch
a stone

goblin

& shapes of thinges

corresponding
of the nursery

gap

like a little doorway
Satan
had beene forgotten

not hastening

as he called it
swift letters

a private mark

goblin

night after night
the starry seas
peopled

is there nothing

even deer

gorge

dewlap
the internal throat

fraternal

to brothers
a brother

without a name

vast districts
of all his brothers

were it possible
we would have facts

things of the open

gentle

the flesh-fly or blue bottle
the smell of warm straw

his fever
a beautiful thread

placed on a hook

travellers

what made them

go

to admit of being put on
sun on water
I shall be twenty-three
the sergeant in going on was shot through the body

extravagance of language

use up
as a lover

'do you go with me?' attend
and take in hand.

to carry one's view backward in time
(an engagement, a promise, an undertaking)
to betray
and no more to be relied upon

the pockets of an elderly gentleman

water

the heavy go of water
I do not think he cares a straw
their lonely cottage

beggar girl

attack, or attempt at
music full of humor
the adjutant wants you.

past, pass

to lose brightness

in various senses
this horse, the
heavy go of the water,
mettle, spirit.

popular religious ballads.

she looked like a boat

she looked like a boat;
one
causes embarrassment,
'rage', a territorial possession.

to forsake

a lamb, a small stone. sing
of a contest, war, to be given up:

pass from mouth to mouth

betake oneself
and go on one's knees:

he has taught that song very prettily
almost without education

to harmonize
backward, backwards;
of the sun, etc.;
to be obscured by a cloud.

laid up with camphor in tissue paper, including his tall hat

he left the sea, having had what amounted to a nervous
    breakdown, 'always thinking of the other ships that
    went up, the bombings and suchlike'.

come, come!

a great desire to be gone
as if it were going to

I will follow you to the world's end,
I am myself very far

more than the age

evidence

there ran such a sea, that we expected, every instant,
the boat would go down

and forget all their mercies

fraught

large memory
griefs
usually by water

in mid water

be sea
schippes with salt

counterfet Gods
all kind of strange beasts

gentle

free from
a medicine:
of a river:
that loved

haswed

marked

or got

or

fer a-wei

or got

or

marked

marked with

or

free

where one wishes;
of a horse
of the wind:
of material things:

go

[bees] are reddy to flye
that when they
they make a great humming
they
from their word
lost
I lost
from their word
I lost him

godwit

obscure

upwards

to render

take him

the common
the Stone
the windings

arrives

go

to break, also to break
the letters betrayed
him

does not care what becomes of him

to sea in her

girl

we could wish
into the world
into the haunts

shelter

dreadful

go

the letters of the alphabet
in rags

wishes   the boundary here

to have been pregnant

and begged
(tale, story)

the world's taken
wind or water
or
church clock

letters of
lilt
(a name

never
a time
to have been pregnant

and never

I lost
they make a great humming

I lost him

grieved
and never
rags
boundary
                    clatter, clatter

the hand went so strangely

give

athirst
many nuns

to the child but fraile
you my sore throat

the washings.... bubbled, subsided, and gave lime

freckle

she was running about

his unrivalled pencil
the firmament

never mind
she so much thirsts for

through the branches fall
the half-clothed branches in the woods

you know I

girth

for God's sake
I clothed

troopers
on the rich grass

within the four seas

seas of fabled
nerve
horse

robes are thrown over them

loosely

seemed
and crossed

draw (a string)
close round

go

the measure I
(a river)

gain

evil
a dancing girl

loss

seven centuries and a half

it is omitted
the battle

devoted cities   whirling wheels

it is not certain

he drewe his swerde and layed about hym

roads or directions

or fish
put her own dress in order
to spare oneself
the wind

if on a pillory
the weather-side of some other vessel

the trenches
scanty sustenance
the gain
the waters

a hundred fights
thick forest
from the sea
that calamity

gap

kill two birds

a way to escape

evil breaking in

from this town a road has been cut

cutting his own fingers

like a little doorway

a private mark

he had beene forgotten

evil breaking in upon us

glide

to the pilot by radar:
a liquid, a stream. keyhole
and the smallest fish.
the young man's shoulder
like something greasy;
unperceived in poetry:
a great dog-fox as red as the fir-stems through which he glides.

give

Nature seems thirsting

and decorated churches

furlong

in the common field

are wanting

I had

forty falls
this noise may be heard

forty poles

space
contains
according to
a brief space

walking this
superficial
blunder

headland

a road our boundary
unenclosed
containing

the land must be cast into another
land lying
a general trench

foes

an equal influence

friend

a hostile meeting was arranged
to a stranger

at a distance
the prisoner will be handed over

keep it
keep it

let him
already fought
of God

never you mind, Mother, just now

in silence of the night
we expect evil
the firmest minds

keep it
or at variance

keep
me again, Mary?

bring ammunition
speaking ill

but at his birth the boy...

she may do you an ill turn
asking leave
implore her

the street is narrow

but at his birth the boy

implore her
Mary

follow

story
>
>opened the door for her in silence
>had been waiting for her

action or an act
which it has set in motion
against which
it has flown

>I used to come to him in the field
>into the path
>hazarding

things altered very much

>we follow'd up the river as we rode

the impulse given

>for wounded deer
>to hold heavy

adhere

and damage any subject
other evidence

>to be a soldier

other stories

> a woman with child
> lighting
> bright and hard

> a person's funeral
> all the days of my life

but, as in war, there must also be
almost faces

> for more than forty years
> these twenty years
> waiting for her

what harm, undone

> waiting for her

story

the calling of a sailor
the door for her in silence

in the field

gibbous

she comes
in a wan decline

and the related
rounded
protuberant

wrasse, a fish
hump
bunch back'd

all your kindred some
is there of all
he dies
in consequence
is there

would vanish away

girl

labouring over a letter

go

claps into light
a birding

after other gods
their collars
loaves and fishes

I came in

let us say no more about it

to disappear
off the hooks
into holes

girlhood
abolished

I lost him

and his flannels shrink
the
weather
good
going everywhere

and went to sea

do let me keep her [the baby]

the weather was constantly

the terror whereof
loaves and fishes

we could not make him understand it

the measure I
(a river)

drawn of a world where all went by chance

parallel with the river
curious observations (like over-small watches)

of a gun: to be fired

I do not want her body

the air remained as dry

of waves, wind, etc.: to subside.

to take in hand
an advanced stage of disease
to take in hand

I
cannot bear
make holes in

who cried
the vessel
for ever where ever

and came down on his knees

I can scarcely
I have resolved
I'm so frightened

and so she went, and she went

we could not make him understand it

dead drunk
the balcony

the women
a begging

the needful workmen

twelve has gone

the clock

amiss, astern, astray

The hand went so strangely
without a burden
I came in
I couldn't possibly tell

what has become of
of a route, etc.
leave a place
baffled

let us say no more about it
people will hate
to disappear

into holes
dull, and long

to make bread for herself
to be carried adrift
to devils
a birding

he went into a railway

himself willing to fight

the enemy
full mourning

embracing you
the woods
Anna, good sister

connected with wire or wire-ropes
in the last twenty years
against my feelings

admit of being sung

said also of the hour

crash, patter, smash

devil's corn
all her colour
skin and bone

if you boil
to a jelly
Mrs. Glasse
to this one girl

his love was not
the history
of treason

his mathematics
the horns

a charming child

fever medicine
a portion
scraped

simple senses
on a wind

      I've gone off him

on one's knees

the contents of the casket

at his legs the little dog
prophecies promysed
reckoned

we saw Paris
collapse

and the sun

God

and little fishes
feast, sight, etc.
from the machine
from a machine

a monstir maid
still cries excellent

circulating libraries

sing
claptraps
sing

girl

she was a dreadful
with red elbows
with intention

another frame

with intention
whose houses
bit their tongues turning

forty years

another frame
nothing at all

she lay in bed
cast down
temporary
of the pavements

pictured in story beginning

we discovered a box
it would be terrible

dancing behind

I have not half done
tragedies
tendencies

handing in his message

solider has been
falls

back on shore
a letter

waits for her

generate

next
these two

in March or April

when he is dead

these two the worlde

pencils
exhaust
all of the sentences of English

monsters
from the agitation of the sea
a mere
where rain was

if a
union of those bodies
fluid
gunpowder
carried to the place
rifle
the water
so many men

these two the worlde

and the diseases
these two the worlde dampned in certainetie

all of the sentences of English and only these

I was

such shadows they

those of waters

furlough

the aged
for another world
beg

amid the hue and cry

outward

go

That when they [bees] are reddy to flye, or going, they
make a great humming.

force

in the possessive
said ships
the man and the girl
a body of

and ruin them

stress of weather:
in the thieving

invisible barrier

of their lives
strangers

infection

there are four groups

play as to show
cause
the enemy is reported
to make force at him with their horns

it does not matter about, no need to care for:
you must render yourself contemptible
proclamations
flowers
bread

to strain
the meaning

i.e., leg biting

you must never be

with a sentence

.

green chess
the sky
the maturity of
which he had occupied.

halve

to divide
Man-slaer
imperfect
like the Moon
the fervid Sun

halfing with God

to halve a hole
to reach it
mangled and
crooked

faithlesse

gentle

half an acre of rocky place

I should take
of you

gibbous

illuminated
is less than
never

kindred

goose

your grandmother

this
ruined

grandmother

this fellow in revenge for this

rope

lapping

gradation

some advances they
enter into the eye

cut-purse
the son attained
moulder away

our tragedy
the sticks of the cage

inform our generals

center of the evil
an orange
prison
green, blue, indigo

their first creation
an insensible passing

his sky will not come right

gentleness

one's inherited
the bearing of armes

in great danger
and flows on silently like a river of oil

violence
(no doubt) is caused, by
home
sloping towards the head
home
measure i' the feet
and in face dysposyd to fyghtyng

draw no lesse then the face

gorge

the water

his slaughter'd army

the water

hanging down to his knees
every sheet of paper occupied

the water which is

men of a certain sort
foul basket
the human face

the water which is supposed to

choke
form an obstruction

which ought not to have been

and dammed the water
we came to where it lay

gap

we swept through another
nets
to spare some men

free

without knots

strange; if strange

a face

girl

years before

she converses with me

fraught

the river stream, her load of water

forget

I haven't written

we had no candles

not
length

though cold

to lose

gorge

doubtful
throat

throttle you
to his knees

what has been swallowed

intended to be swallowed

the human face [is]
whirlpool
sulphur smoke

broken
from the drawing broken

and
necessary to carry

we came to where it lay

Note on the typeface:

This book is set in Imprint, the same typeface used in the most recent print edition of the *Oxford English Dictionary*, the second, published in 1989. Imprint was designed in 1912, and was the first typeface developed specifically for mechanical composition. Though editors are at work on the third edition of the dictionary, that edition will be published electronically, and the second edition will most likely be the last print edition of the *OED*.

Laura Walker is the author of *bird book* (Shearsman Books, 2011), *rimertown/ an atlas* (UC Press, 2008), and *swarm lure* (Battery Press, 2004), and the chapbook *bird book* (Albion Books, 2010). Her poetry has also appeared in *VOLT, Switchback, Ambush, Thermos,* and *Fact-Simile,* as well as other journals. She grew up in North Carolina and now lives in Berkeley, California, where she teaches creative writing.

OTHER POETRY TITLES
FROM APOGEE PRESS

Maxine Chernoff
Among the Names
The Turning

Valerie Coulton
The Cellar Dreamer
open book
passing world pictures

Tsering Wangmo Dhompa
In the Absent Everyday
My rice tastes like the lake
Rules of the House

Kathleen Fraser
Discrete Categories Forced into
Coupling

Paul Hoover
Edge and Fold

Alice Jones
Gorgeous Mourning
Plunge

Stefanie Marlis
cloudlife
fine

Edward Kleinschmidt Mayes
Speed of Life

Pattie McCarthy
bk of (h)rs
Table Alphabetical of Hard
Words
Verso

Denise Newman
Human Forest
Wild Goods

Elizabeth Robinson
Also Known As
Apostrophe
Apprehend

Edward Smallfield
equinox
The Pleasures of C

Cole Swensen
Oh

Truong Tran
dust and conscience
four letter words
placing the accents
within the margin

**TO ORDER OR FOR MORE
INFORMATION GO TO
WWW.APOGEEPRESS.COM**